LINICI

PASTELS

PASTELS

Ian Sidaway

SUNBURST BOOKS

This edition first published in 1996 by
Sunburst Books,
Kiln House,
210 New Kings Road,
London SW6 4NZ

© Sunburst Books 1996

The right of Ian Sidaway to be identified as the author of this work has been
asserted by him in accordance with the Copyright, Designs and Patents Act 1988.

ISBN 1 85778 218 6

Printed and bound in China

C O N T E N T S

INTRODUCTION

PASTEL IS A RELATIVELY modern medium: black and red crayons were made in stone age times whilst hard chalks and crayons in the limited palette of white, black and red were developed and have been in use since the late 15th century. However pastels as we know and use them today, in a limited (by today's standards) but relatively comprehensive range of colours, only came into use around 250 years ago.

Despite pastel's fragility, it rapidly gained in popularity, its potential being exploited and explored by artists such as Rosalba Carriera (1675-1757), Quinten de La Tour (1704-1788) and Chardin (1699-1779). Pastels popularity waned during the first half of the 19th century along with the demand for portraits, but the medium was seized on and its strengths immediately recognised by the Impressionists. Edgar Degas (1834-1917) developed techniques that were far removed from the delicate portrait and landscape work that the medium had been used for previously.

Degas and the other Impressionists were quick to see how the purity of colour and the immediacy of the pastel technique made it a medium that suited their ideas concerning colour and light. New techniques were utilised and invented that did away with the subtle blending that had been used in the past. Artists began using confident strokes of bright colour which were laid next to each other and allowed to interact visually and mix optically or they used broad flat areas of colour contained by fluid, flowing line work.

Pastel is unique; it is a dry painting medium that needs neither the addition of water nor turpentine. Pastel colour is colour in its purest form - unadulterated by additives or diluted with liquid media. The effect of working with a pastel is immediate as the colour seems to flow from the very fingertips and the colours, far from being pale and insipid, are invariably surprisingly strong and bright.

Perhaps the one thing that really sets pastels apart from other media, and which requires from the artist some confidence and perhaps a certain degree of recklessness, is the fact that pastels cannot be mixed on a palette prior to being applied to the support compounding the immediate nature of the medium.

Despite all of its attractions and potential, pastel, for one reason or another, has unfairly been saddled as a medium used predominantly by rather amateur artists. Perhaps given today's concerns with finance, value for money and longevity the fragile pastel is seen as a risky thing for the artist to invest his or her valuable time in. But then given the current rebirth and interest in good figurative painting, pastel as a traditional medium may yet begin to find its way back into more artists' studios.

This book serves as an introduction to some of the many pastel techniques that are in common practice as well as a few that are not. Only dry pigment pastels are dealt with here and not wax or oil pastels that, whilst similar, do require a slightly different approach. After the chapter dealing with equipment and materials you will find a chapter that shows techniques, many of which are used in the projects throughout the book. It is my belief that practising, experimenting and becoming familiar with these techniques, in isolation and without becoming involved in making pictures, will help give confidence in handling the materials.

The projects vary in complexity, each one combining a range of techniques with specific picture making principals. You will be shown how to prepare supports and how to work on different surfaces. How to build up paintings in layers, how to use different types of pastel and how to use fixative creatively. You will also be shown several alternative paintings and drawings that deal with and solve similar problems to those dealt with in the project paintings. Whilst you are working it should be born in mind that there is no right or wrong way of using pastel, it is a versatile and seductive medium that can be adapted and used in a surprisingly wide variety of ways.

MATERIALS AND EQUIPMENT

Types of paper and board

The quality, texture or tooth, tone and colour of the support you choose to work on can make the difference between success and failure, so the choice should be given careful thought and consideration. The range of paper and board available is wide and varied and paper is expensive - so making the wrong choice not only makes the drawing process more difficult it can also leave a hole in the wallet. Beginners are often bewildered by what is on offer and find it difficult to decide which paper or board it is best to use. When choosing paper for pastel work the three most important considerations that need to be matched to your subject and style of working are the tooth, which is the texture of the paper; the colour, is it warm, cool or neutral and the right choice for the subject; and finally the tone, or how light or dark the colour is.

Pastel takes best on paper that has at least some tooth or texture: on very smooth paper pastel tends to slide over the surface and the pigment dust is spread evenly and clogs up what little texture the surface has very quickly, resulting in a thick, impasto layer of pigment making it difficult to overlay more pastel. The rougher papers shave off more pastel from the stick but the dust builds up more slowly on the coarser textured surface and adheres more firmly, which enables more layers to be overworked before the support surface becomes completely clogged. The pronounced tooth on the rougher papers shows through the work giving a sparkling, broken colour effect and is one of the reasons why careful thought should be given to the colour and tone of your support.

Mi-Teintes and Ingres are types of pastel paper that are available in a wide range of tones and colours from several different manufacturers. The better known ones being Canson, Fabriano, Sennelier, Tumba, and Daler-Rowney. The Mi-Teintes papers have a more pronounced tooth, not unlike fine canvas, whilst the Ingres paper can be recognised by the hundreds of feint parallel lines that run across its surface. Either side of the paper can be used, one side you will find is slightly rougher than the other, the choice is yours. Pastel papers are usually of medium weight falling between 90gsm and 160gsm, lighter weight papers suitable for pastel are available but these can cockle when fixative is applied so they are best used for sketches or, if used for more important work, it may be advisable to stretch them beforehand in the same way that you would stretch watercolour paper. Pastel, when used on thinner papers, can also show up any imperfections or marks in the drawing board so place few extra sheets of paper beneath the one you are working on to act as padding and prevent this from happening.

Pastel boards are available but in a limited range of colours, the boards are simply made by mounting pastel paper onto a cardboard backing. It is a relatively easy process to make your own. Cut a piece of cardboard to the size you want the painting to be, cut a piece of pastel paper a little larger than the cardboard, with a large flat brush apply a water-based glue evenly and thinly over both the board and the paper, then align the paper along one edge of the board and lay it onto the board smoothing it level as you go. Once the paper is down, smooth it flat and remove any air bubbles by rubbing over the surface with a soft cloth working from the middle outwards. Once the paper is firmly in position the edges can be trimmed with a sharp knife.

Several other papers and boards also give ideal surfaces on which to work, a range of pastel boards and papers are available manufactured by Schmincke, known as Sansfix they have a very, fine, granular, sand-like surface that is very pleasant to work on. A similar pastel board is available from Frisk. Velour, or flocked, papers are like velvet and take pastel very easily but are difficult to fix as the velvety surface comes away from the backing paper if wet, so drawings are prone to damage unless stored very carefully or framed immediately. Very fine sandpaper, sometimes known as flour paper, can be purchased at some hardware shops, this makes a wonderful surface on which to work but unlike artist's papers is not acid free so your drawings may deteriorate with time. 'Not' and 'Rough' surface watercolour paper can also be used and although these are white, which is not a desirable colour to work on in pastel, they can be stretched and toned with watercolour or thin acrylic paint to any colour that you wish.

Canvas and fine muslin can also be used, these can either be glued to hardboard or a thin sheet of medium density fibre-board (MDF) or alternatively, for canvas, stretched as for oil painting but with a sheet of cardboard at the back between the canvas and the stretchers. One advantage of using canvas is that, should you wish to, pastel works of a substantial size can be produced. Do not use an oil based primer but a water based acrylic one. The desired ground colour can be added to the primer using acrylic paint or added as a separate coat once the primer is totally dry. The grade or texture of the canvas you choose will very much depend on the desired result, but for most work a fine linen or 10oz cotton duck should suffice.

One of the most satisfying surfaces to work on are marble-dust boards, these are not commercially available but are very easy to make - the process is described later in the book.

The colour and tone of the paper is important for several reasons, pastel rarely completely covers the support and if you use a white paper you will find that you are desperately trying to obliterate every bit of white with pigment - unless you are painting a snow scene, and even then you may find that a blue paper works better. Choosing a paper colour that contrasts with your subject will often enrich and intensify the colours that you use, whilst choosing a paper that harmonises with your subject can cut down on work, making it easier to asses and match colours and tonal values. Strong, strident coloured papers are more difficult to use as they easily overpower the softer, more subtle pastel colours. It is perhaps best to stick with the more muted, neutral browns, ochres, greens and greys which more closely echo those colours seen in nature.

The tonal value of a colour is judged to be correct by comparing it against the tonal value of the colours that surround it, that is why working onto a light or white support can be difficult. Working on a mid-tone paper allows you to judge both the lighter and darker tones more accurately. Dark tone papers can emphasise the lighter tones whilst a light paper will work in the opposite way and make the darker tones and colours appear stronger.

Pastels

Three distinct types of pastel are available, these are soft pastels, hard pastels and pastel pencils, all three can be used freely, one with the other, as can different makes. Pastels are made by mixing dry, raw pigment with a binder and preservative, only enough binder is used to hold the particles of pigment together which is why pastel colours appear to be so strong. Different types of pigments require different types and amounts of binder, these include gum tragacanth, various resins, starch and milk. Some old recipes for making pastels even advise on using stale beer.

Because pastel is a dry medium and the colours cannot be mixed prior to being applied, manufacturers offer a wide range of colour, tints and tones. Talens, Schmincke, Sennelier, Daler-Rowney, Faber-Castell, Grumbacher, Unison, Conte, Caren D'ache, Carb-Othello, to name but a few, all offer ranges of soft, hard and pastel pencils that together give a choice of over 600 different colours and tints, Sennelier, one of the main pastel manufacturers offers an assortment of 525.

Soft pastels offer the artist the largest range of colours; these are round and fragile and arrive wrapped in paper. Whenever possible, unless you need to use the pastel on its side, remove only enough paper to enable the pastel to make its mark, as the paper not only helps prevent the stick from crumbling it also keeps it clean. Very little binder is used in the manufacture of soft pastels, which is why they are soft. However soft is a relative term, as you will notice that the degree of softness varies from one brand to another, as it does with different colours.

Soft pastel colours are graded as to their tonal value, unfortunately this grading system differs from brand to brand, with some ranges carrying as many as ten shades of certain colours. Put simply, each colour can be found in its purest, strongest form together with different shades and tints of the same colour. The darker shades mix pure pigment with black, whilst the lighter shades are mixed by adding white chalk.

Soft pastels, like paints, are graded for permanence however most offer good resistance to the effects of light and fading.

Hard pastels are square, they have a higher binder content than the round soft pastels making them firmer. They can be sharpened to a point using a sharp craft knife or razor blade, which makes them ideal for drawing and work where sharp, fine lines are needed. They can be used by themselves or with soft pastels to tighten up and pull slightly fuzzy areas into sharp focus or they can be broken into small pieces and used on their side to block in areas of flat colour. Because hard pastels, when used, shed considerably less pigment than soft pastels they can be used to establish a composition without fear of clogging up the tooth of the support which could make further applications of

softer pastels difficult. Hard pastels are not available in as wide a range of shades and tints as soft pastels but the colours that are available are carefully chosen.

Hard pastels can be blended on the support with fingers or torchon, they can be optically mixed by hatching or other means, and glazing colours lightly one on top of the other is easy and straightforward.

Pastel pencils are, as the name suggests, thin strips of hard pastel encased in wood, because of this they are clean to work with. The range of colours echo those found for hard pastels and like them they can be sharpened to a point and are an excellent choice for fine linear work and cross hatching. Be gentle with pastel pencils, if they are dropped the pastel strip will break making them impossible to sharpen.

Pastels are sold in sets or can be purchased individually. Sets are available consisting of anything from 12 basic colours up to the full range. A basic set whilst providing a useful introduction to the medium may not provide the best selection for your chosen subjects. You may find it better to buy an empty box, these are available to accommodate various numbers of pastels, and fill it with your own carefully chosen range of colours. A useful tip is, no matter what spectrum of colours you select, try to purchase at least three tones, a light, medium and dark in each one.

Pastels do not stay in the same clean, pristine condition they are bought in for very long, they wear down, sometimes at an alarming rate, and pieces become broken off. As you replace used pastels you will find that you are collecting a lot of bits, these are all usable and useful so should never be thrown away. Artists who use pastels a great deal collect hundreds of broken and partly used sticks so keep them in separate boxes according to individual colours or colour groups (ultramarines, cadmium reds, greys and so on) such a systematic approach not only stops the pastels becoming dirty with other colours, it also makes for ease of use and helps you keep track of colours and whether or not any need replacing.

Pastels do become dirty, an easy way to clean them is to three quarter fill a jam jar with ground rice or, if unavailable, ordinary white rice and place in any dirty pastels, shake the jar for a while and the slight abrasive action of the rice will remove the dirty outer layer of the pastels leaving them nice and clean.

As you work, selecting pastels from your box or boxes, put the pastels you are using to one side and do not replace them until you have finished work as it can be both exasperating and time consuming to keep re-finding specific colours and shades when absorbed in an inspired flurry of creativity.

Erasures

Pastel, prior to fixing, can easily be erased in a number of ways. A soft brush or rag flicked over a surface will remove a large amount of pastel dust and lighten an image considerably. Traditionally a birds wing was used and whilst difficult, if not impossible, to find in an art shop today you can easily obtain your own by buying an unprepared duck or game bird from your local butcher. White bread rubbed gently over the paper also cleans and erases pastel from large areas remarkably well. Fine, hard bristle brushes can be used in confined and precise areas as can cottonwool buds or a clean torchon. A sharp knife held at right angles to the support and pulled across the surface will also successfully remove excess pastel and can be used to remove heavy build-ups prior to erasing proper.

Some conventional erasures need be used with care, plastic and India rubber erasures should be avoided as they become clogged with pigment very quickly and can push the pigment deep into the tooth making it very difficult, sometimes impossible, to remove. The putty rubber is, as its name suggests, soft and malleable. It can be used for cleaning up large areas or moulded to a point for erasing small precise areas. As it becomes dirty a fresh clean profile can be found simply by cutting away the dirty side with a sharp knife.

Erasing, however, should not be thought of as simply a way of getting rid of mistakes but as a means of making marks that can add interest and surface quality to overworked areas or as a means to lighten tones, make patterns and soften, or blend, crisp edges.

Knives and Sharpeners

Soft pastels can be sharpened very carefully with a sharp knife but the point disappears more or less immediately the pastel is used. Hard pastels and pastel pencils sharpen better using a knife or a conventional pencil sharpener, a point can also be given to hard pastels by rubbing them onto fine sandpaper.

Fixative

Pastel paintings are very fragile and unless fixed, smudge very easily, so they need to be stored with great care or framed immediately. Fixative is a varnish that, as it dries hardens, fixing the pigment to the support. The use of fixative, whether to use it or not, is an ongoing debate amongst pastel artists. Many consider that it does the work no favours at all, destroying tonal values, darkening the colour and removing the sparkle and brilliance that is characteristic of traditional pastel painting. I use fixative freely as the painting progresses both to fix areas of work that I intend to repaint with more layers of pastel and to intentionally darken areas of colour so as to enable me to extend the tonal range of the colours I have at my disposal.

Fixative affects certain colours more than others and the difference between an area that has been fixed and an area that remains unfixed is especially noticeable where lighter colours have been used and, with heavy fixing, white can almost disappear completely. These problems can be overcome by fixing the painting just before it is completed, then finishing with layers of unfixed colour that will retain their brilliance and freshness. A painting does not have to be fixed all over, by cutting or tearing paper masks it is possible to fix selected areas leaving those areas of colour that seem prone to more dramatic changes untouched. Furthermore, erasing sometimes flattens and smooths out the tooth of the support, making it reluctant to accept further pastel, here a light spray of fixative prior to any reworking can solve the problem.

Fixative is available in aerosol cans or as bottles of liquid for which you will need a diffuser. To spray a painting first tap the support to dislodge any loose dust then secure the painting to a drawing board and prop it vertically on the easel or up against a wall. Test the spray before you use it on the painting as occasionally they fail to atomise and a jet, rather than a spray, is discharged which could spoil your work. Hold the can at least 12in (30cm) away from the work and steadily direct the spray back and forth across the painting. Using fixative liquid and a diffuser is a little more difficult as regulating the flow of air and so the amount of fixative dispersed, takes a little practice, but the principle remains the same.

An alternative method is to spray fixative onto the back or reverse side of the paper, if sufficient is used it should soak through and wet the pastel dust holding it in place as it dries. I have never found this method to be particularly satisfactory but I know of people who swear by it.

Drawing Boards, Easels and Sundry Equipment

A good drawing board is essential, choose one that is large enough to accommodate the largest size sheet of paper that you are likely to use, few things are as irksome as trying to work on a sheet of paper that is too large for the drawing board. But remember that as you grow in experience so may the size of your paintings. It may make good sense to have two boards, a smaller, lighter board for working on location and a larger, heavier board for more ambitious drawings done in the home or studio. Drawing boards can be bought from an art suppliers or made cheaply from medium density fibre-board. Several boards can be cut from a standard size sheet of MDF in sizes that match the paper sizes that you use most frequently.

Pastels are best done with the support vertical as this allows excess pastel dust to fall harmlessly to the floor, rather than lie on the support surface where the artist tends to blow it away, dispersing it into the air. Whilst strict manufacturing regulations keep harmful, toxic pigments to a bare minimum, breathing pastel dust is best avoided, as is breathing any other kind of dust. An easel allows the work to be kept vertical and can be adjusted to height allowing the artist to work either standing up or sitting down. The easel must be stable as pastel work calls for a fair degree of pressure to be applied so the easel must keep the drawing board and the support in place. You will also need a table, or trolley, to hold your pastels and any additional equipment. This needs to be positioned close to the easel and if it has wheels making it easy to move, so much the better.

A mahl stick has a long handle with a soft, usually chamois covered pad at one end. It is used by holding the handle in one hand and resting the pad on the edge of the drawing board or part of the easel. The other hand, holding the pastel, can then be rested on the long handle and steadied whilst being kept clear of the picture surface, so preventing it from becoming smudged or smeared.

Torchons or tortillons are soft paper rolls that are used to blend colours together; you will find it makes good sense to have a few and keep one for blues, one for reds and so on as you can very easily contaminate a colour by using a torchon that has been used to blend a different colour. Torchons are good for small areas but for the most part fingers are better. Paper is best attached to your board with heavy clips, one at each corner. Drawing or push-pins can be used but avoid using tape as it can tear the surface of the paper.

TECHNIQUES

TECHNIQUES ARE THOSE MARKS and effects that can be achieved using a chosen medium. By having a broad knowledge and working repertoire of such techniques the artist is liberated to concentrate on the content of his, or her, work.

Many techniques are remarkably simple but in order to achieve them and use them successfully they need to be executed in a seemingly effortless and smooth manner. This requires practice and it is my belief that any time spent handling and experimenting with your materials will help you to become familiar with the technical skills that pastel painting requires.

Learning about techniques is cumulative, one method often leads the way to another - and many are but simple variations on each other. It is not obligatory or even desirable to have an image in mind, just to use and experiment with the materials themselves. Working abstractly in this way channels more thought and concentration into the mark making process. This unconscious control of the medium enables the artist to turn attention to colour, form, perspective, composition and other fundamental principles that are central to good pastel work.

Pastel is a unique medium as it sits astride a fence that has drawing on one side and painting on the other: it leans toward and owes much to both disciplines, and in doing so it borrows and combines techniques from both.

Pastels require focus as the medium is not an easy one and can very easily get the better of you. This is not to say it is as dependent for success on technique as is watercolour, nevertheless like watercolour it does require a certain amount of planning and forethought. This coupled with the right techniques make pastels surprisingly versatile and capable of precise photographic realism, colourful impressionistic work or large colour field abstracts - in other words, whatever takes your fancy.

The Techniques

▲

Presenting the pastel end on to the support will give a mark - the thickness and density of which can be varied by turning the stick as it wears and by varying the pressure with which it is applied.

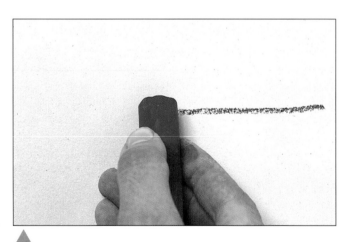

▲

Holding the stick in the same way but pulling it sideways across the support will present less of the pastel to the support, so making a thin linear mark that, as before, can be lightened or darkened simply by applying more or less pressure.

Drawing the pastel sideways across the support leaves a broad band of even colour; the density of pigment can be altered by varying the pressure and the speed with which the pastel is applied. By using this technique very large areas of colour can be blocked in remarkably quickly.

Turning the pastel on its axis as it is pulled across the support gives a fluid flowing band of colour that will vary in thickness.

Large areas of flat colour are built up by using the pastel on its side. The required density is better

achieved by working several thin layers one on top of the other: the first layer is applied using broad parallel strokes using the full length of the pastel, the second layer is then applied at right angles to the first.

Alternatively in order to achieve a more random effect, work the pastel in all and every direction with each layer. If you wish, each layer can be given a spray of fixative to bind it to the support.

By using short heavy strokes, small blobs or blocks of pure colour are placed next to each other that, when viewed from a suitable distance, optically fuse to create an overall tone or colour that is a mixture of the colours used. This optical mixing was the principle that was used by the Pointillists. It was known by the artists who practised it as Divisionism and is a technique perfectly suited to pastel work as all colour mixing takes place on the support. Entire paintings can be executed using the technique or it can be used in tandem with other techniques. Turning the pastel - altering the angle that makes the mark and varying the spacing - makes irregularities in the dot pattern, so preventing them from looking too mechanical.

Hatching uses a series of parallel lines to give an impression of an overall tone or colour. Hatching is essentially a linear technique, the colours used are left unblended. By altering the distance between the lines, the depth of colour used and the thickness of the lines, the tone can be made lighter or darker and the colour more or less saturated. By steadily widening the distance between the lines, tones and colours can be made to fade light to dark. Hatched lines can be short or long, thick or thin, sharp or vague, they can also be curved so they are seen to flow around the form following the direction of its surfaces.

Two or more colours can be hatched together creating colour that will mix together optically when viewed from a distance. Hatching large areas in one direction only, needs to be done with care, the painting can easily look lopsided as the eye tends to be drawn off in the direction that the hatched lines are running. Hatched areas offer a lively contrast and can look considerably more vibrant and interesting than flat, uniform areas of colour.

Cross-hatching is also a way of building an area of tone or colour which, like hatching, is a linear technique. With cross-hatching the tone and colour is built up by overlaying hatched lines, each layer hatched at a different angle to the previous one. Hatching is an easily controlled technique and it is possible to achieve extremely subtle and intricate

variations of tone and colour intensity simply by varying the density of line.

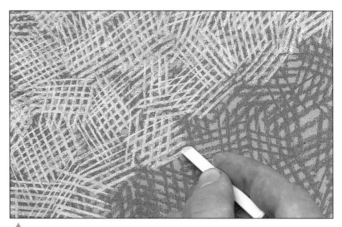

Coloured cross-hatching is carried out in the same way - however for each layer a different colour is used. As with hatching these layers of different colour mix optically when viewed from a distance. Cross-hatching can be done straight onto the support or over previously worked surfaces. Both hatching techniques are extremely useful for reviving tired, flat areas of colour and adding vigour to the work.

Scribbling is a simple and quick way of laying down a tone or texture. It enables the creation of subtle areas of colour and tone of varying density and strength to be established quickly. Large uniform areas of tone can look flat and uninteresting, whereas scribbled areas look fresh and alive. You can build an area up by covering it several times over using more or less the same light pressure, or by applying more pressure cover the area in one dark layer. If you apply heavy pressure to a pastel it will wear down very quickly and make a very distinct, unsubtle mark. Hold the pastel near the lower end when using heavy pressure or it will break. Holding the pastel higher forces you to apply less pressure and so make lighter marks.

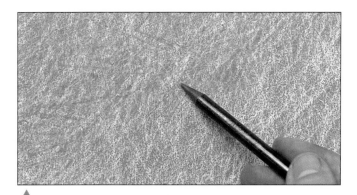

An area of colour that has been fixed can be scribbled over with an ordinary pencil, graphite stick or charcoal - this will have the effect of knocking back the colour or tone making it less strident or darker.

When scribbling tone or colour always vary the direction of the strokes by altering the angle of the drawing implement or, if you are working flat, by turning the paper or board.

Scumbling is achieved by working lightly with a blunt tip or broken piece of pastel in a loose, haphazard, roughly circular motion over another colour. The pastel is applied in such a way as to leave gaps that will allow the previous layer of colour to show through. Here a dark colour is scumbled over a lighter colour.

Here a light colour is scumbled over a darker colour, layer upon layer can be applied in the same way. If you

fix between layers the colours will stay separate, otherwise as each layer is applied it will pick up and move the pigment that is left by previous layers, blending slightly with them. The effect will be less crisp than if fixative had been used. By choosing colours or tones that are close to one another they will mix optically giving a subtle shimmering surface that would be impossible to achieve by overlaying flat colours.

Sgraffito is a method whereby a layer of pastel is scratched or scraped into using a sharp implement, so exposing what is beneath, this could be the support or another layer of pastel. The word Sgraffito comes from the Italian word *graffiare* which means to scratch. The underlayer must be consolidated either by fixing or by being well rubbed into the tooth of the support. Alternatively, the lower layers could be a coloured ground of acrylic paint or gouache. The over layer should be applied thickly using soft pastel and must not be fixed or rubbed into the support but should remain untouched. Any sharp instrument can be used to scratch through to the lower layer, as can your fingernails or even sandpaper. If you are working on paper take care not to tear or cut right through it.

To achieve a broken colour effect, short strokes of colour are applied so that they sit unmixed, next to each other. When viewed from a suitable distance the colours optically fuse and blend, whilst seen close to, the surface stays lively and fresh. The technique is not unlike that used by the Pointillists, the achieved effect is similar but the pastel marks are more fluid and irregular, often following along in the direction of the contours of your subject.

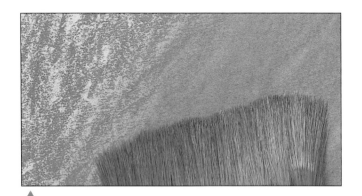

A large, flat, soft bristle brush is useful for blending and softening large areas of pastel. Use the brush gently to spread and remove excess dry pigment, or used more vigorously and with more pressure it will push the colour deep into the texture of the support making it an ideal technique for consolidating a coloured ground. Smaller, bristle oil painting brushes can be utilised in the same way to blend smaller, more intricate or highly detailed areas.

Blending together two colours to give a subtle graduation one to the other can be achieved by using the finger and it is easy to vary and regulate the pressure needed to accomplish the task.

Take care to wash your hands well before working with pastel to avoid getting any grease on the support which will make the pastel difficult to adhere. However when working with pastels the hands do become dusty and dry very quickly, which will at least dry up any perspiration or greasiness.

The finger is again used, this time to quickly rough

blend broad strokes of light pastel applied over a darker colour. Again using just the right pressure is important, the intention is not to flatten out the colour but to vary the pressure, softening and blending the colour - in some places more than in others. This gives a subtle, undulating effect to the colour that is more interesting than the same colour rendered featureless and flat.

The torchon or tortillon is also used to blend or consolidate colour by pushing it deep into the tooth or textured surface of the support. Tortillons are available with fine points that make them useful for blending intricate detail and working in small areas that are too big for the finger or a brush. Torchons very quickly become contaminated with colour and cannot be washed clean like fingers. To clean torchons and tortillons either peel away the dirty paper or rub the dirty end against fine sandpaper.

The putty or kneadable rubber can be used to remove

thin layers of pastel but thicker layers will clog the eraser very quickly. Thick pastel should be removed by scraping it from the support with a single edged razorblade or a sharp scalpel blade.

A far more efficient means of erasing larger areas of colour, (as long as the pastel has not been applied too densely or thickly), is to use soft, white bread. The bread collects the pigment dust as it is rubbed over the surface, the crumbs are then blown away leaving the surface remarkably clean.

Hard pastel is best used underneath soft pastel. Used over the top the rather softer, thicker layer of pigment prevents the harder pastel from leaving much of a mark. Hard pastels deposit less pigment dust, so do not clog the tooth and texture of the support as quickly as soft pastels; when used with light pressure they also leave lighter marks. When the intention is to work in several layers this can be of great benefit, establishing the composition and blocking in approximate colours and tones with the less comprehensive range of hard pastels, then reworking and finishing the work with the wider range of softer pastels.

Glazing is a traditional oil painting technique where thin layers of transparent colour are laid one on top of the other, each layer modifying and altering the one

beneath. The technique can be used just as successfully with pastels, although hard pastels are best. Used on their side and with a light pressure they deposit a thin layer of colour that allows the previous layer, or layers, to be seen. Here a yellow pastel is glazed over a darker red to achieve a light orange, had the red been glazed over the yellow the resulting orange would have been darker, or more red, as the top colour will always read the stronger.

Small pieces of pastel that are too small to be held should be saved as they can be ground into dust and used for toning grounds. The pastels can be pounded into dust by placing the pieces in a mortar and pestle or by hitting them gently with a hammer. Use either pastels that are all of one colour to give an overall uniform colour or mix pastels of different colours to give an interesting multicoloured effect. Sprinkle the dust onto the support then distribute it thinly and evenly over the surface, rub it deep into the tooth and remove any excess dust with a brush or by tapping the back of the support and then fix.

By placing your paper support over a textured surface such as bark, rough grained wood, wicker or stone and rubbing a pastel over the paper, an image of the texture below is transferred onto the paper. This technique is known as 'frottage'. The technique can be used literally, for instance to create the texture and pattern of a real piece of wood onto a painting of a

still life standing on a wooden table, the wood grain representing the wood grain of the table. Or it can be used more abstractly, simply to create textures that are then used as part of the representation of other, unrelated subjects.

ened to a point can catch on the mask edge pulling it up or tearing it, which can spoil the desired effect.

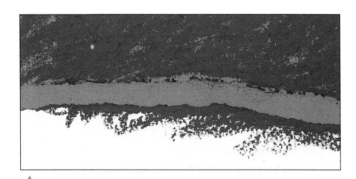

In order to work up to an edge with an area of tone or colour and give that edge a distinct quality, a piece of paper can be torn or cut to shape and placed on the drawing to act as a mask. Hold the mask carefully so that it does not slip, the pastel is worked over the desired area as well as over the edge of the mask. When the mask is removed you will be left with an edge that is difficult to achieve by other means.

Pastels are soluble in water and white spirit or turpentine. The pigments darken noticeably when water is applied but dry to their original colour. When turpentine or white spirit is used the colour becomes darker and richer staying that way once dry. When using washes work either on stretched paper, card or prepared marble-boards. Do not use any kind of liquid on velour paper, sandpaper or prepared pastel boards as the surface textures will be dissolved and the support ruined. The technique can be used to lay a coloured ground or to blend and consolidate the underpainting either in its entirety or selectively, leaving some areas untouched.

A crisp straight edge can be achieved by using a ruler, card or paper as a mask, working up to it in the same way as before. When using thin materials like paper, care should be taken not to work too energetically as hard pastels and pastel pencils that have been sharp-

Soft pastels are best sharpened with a sharp knife or razorblade, however the effect is short-lived as the point will wear down almost immediately. Hard pastels sharpen better and retain their point much longer; they can be sharpened with a scalpel, razorblade, pencil sharpener or simply by rubbing the pastel on sandpaper. Pastel pencils sharpen easily, using any of the ordinary sharpening techniques. Because the pastel strip is relatively soft treat pastel pencils with care, don't drop them or the strip will shatter inside the wooden case making it impossible to sharpen them without pieces persistently breaking off.

PREPARING A MARBLE DUST BOARD

PASTELS WORK BEST on a surface that has a slight tooth or texture and one of the most satisfying surfaces to work on is a rigid board that has been prepared using marble dust. The beauty of this kind of surface is it can be tailor-made to suit your needs, size, shape, colour and degree of tooth can all be varied and adjusted accordingly.

The dust can be applied to the board in one of several ways, either mixing it into a tint made with water and acrylic paint or by simply sprinkling the dust onto the board and spraying the surface with fixative, more tooth is added simply by sprinkling more dust onto the board and refixing. Alternatively the dust can be mixed with gesso and paint, which is the method I use.

You will need a sheet of hardboard or thin MDF (medium density fibre-board) that has been cut to size and the edges sanded smooth, acrylic paint for the desired ground colour, acrylic gesso, marble dust and water.

Use acrylic paint colour for the ground and mix it up in a container straight from the tube without any water, this will ensure that you get no lumps of unmixed colour. Add a little water and mix again, keep mixing and adding water a little at a time, until you think that you have enough. Keep the colour strong as it will lighten enormously when added to the white gesso mix.

Pour sufficient acrylic gesso into a container and whilst stirring add water until it reaches a thin creamy consistency.

Use a clean flat decorating brush and apply the mixture to the board using random brush strokes to get a flat finish. Once this is completely dry give the board a second and if necessary a third coat. Allow the board to dry well before starting work. Any mixture that is left over can be stored until needed again, in an air-tight container. You may find it makes sense to prepare several boards at once rather than one at a time.

Sprinkle in and stir well a dessert-spoonful of marble dust, the exact amount you need depends on how much gesso you have mixed and how rough you want the surface to be. By testing the mixture periodically on a piece of board you should be able to gauge whether or not you need to add any more dust.

Pour in and stir the mixed acrylic paint well. Notice how much the white gesso lightens up the paint, you can mix up and add more colour to the mix to darken it further or alternatively if you desire a very dark tint for the ground, wait until the coats of gesso are dry and apply a wash of dilute colour.

COLOUR

UNLIKE OIL, WATERCOLOUR or other painting materials which require a liquid medium or vehicle to suspend the pigment in, pastel is dry. Wet media can be mixed, modified and altered on a palette prior to being applied to the support - pastel colours can only be mixed on the support. For this reason pastel manufacturers try to remove the need for excessive mixing by supplying the artist with a large range of colours.

With over 600 pastel colours to choose from this gives the artist a wide choice. Mixing takes place on the actual support by glazing colours one over the other, blending, optical mixing, cross-hatching and other techniques. But the intention should always be to keep mixing to a minimum, so preserving the purity of pastel colour. This may infer that in order to work successfully with pastel the artist needs a complete range of colours - in reality this is far from the case. With time and practice it becomes possible to achieve a great deal with relatively few colours.

Artists also tend to specialise in one particular area, this means someone whose work is predominantly concerned with the landscape may amass a large collection of greens, blues and browns but very few pinks and reds, alternatively a portraitist would not need too many blues or greens. However, a basic understanding of colour theory can still be of great help, as the same colour principals apply.

Red, yellow and blue are the primary colours, they cannot be mixed from other colours, hence their collective name. Red and yellow make orange, yellow and blue make green, and blue and red make purple or violet, these mixed colours are known as secondaries. But as a glance at a paint colour chart will show there are many different tones within the various reds, yellows and blues and the secondary colours obtained will depend very much on which of these primaries are used. The same is true of the tertiary colours, these are those colours that fall between the primaries and the secondaries. They are made by mixing an equal amount of a primary colour with an equal amount of the secondary next to it to obtain a red-orange, orange-yellow, yellow-green, green-blue, blue-violet, and violet-red.

All colours are considered to be either warm or cool: the warm colours are red, orange and yellow, the cool colours are green, blue and violet. However, the terms 'warm' and 'cool' are relative as all colours have a warm and cool variant, there are warm reds, such as cadmium which have a yellow bias and cool reds, like alizarin crimson, which have a blue bias. To confuse the issue further a colour that is seen as warm in isolation can appear cool when seen next to a warmer variant of a similar colour. This warm-cool colour relationship is very important and can be put to good use, especially when painting the landscape, as warm colours seem to visually advance and cool colours appear to recede.

Complementary colours are those colours that fall opposite one another on the colour wheel. One colour will always have a warm bias while the other will have a cool bias. Hence red is the complementary of green and orange is the complementary of blue, these colour opposites are known as 'complementary pairs' and have a very special relationship. When placed next to each other complementary pairs have the effect of enhancing or intensifying each othe

The colour wheel shows the primary, secondary and tertiary colours, the 'cool' colours are violet, blue and green, the 'warm' colours are yellow, orange and red.

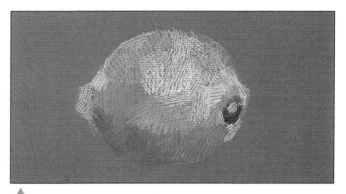

Here the colour is mixed by working in flat glazes.

Fixing noticeably darkens colour and can be used to good advantage by extending a colours' tonal range.

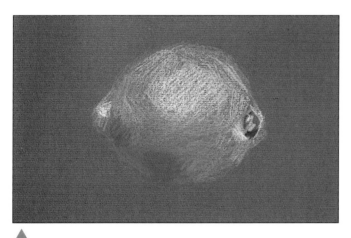

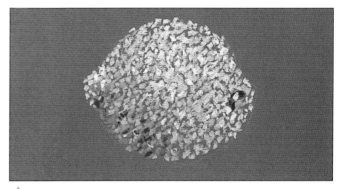

If small dots of pastel are applied next to each other the colour will mix optically when viewed from a distance.

Here the pastels are scribbled delicately over each other.

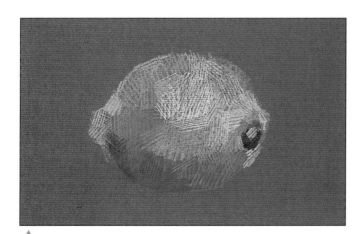

The colour of the support has a marked effect on the perception of a colour.

Colour is applied and mixed by building up cross-hatching.

A NOTE ON COLOURS USED
THROUGHOUT THE BOOK

The grading of pastel colour and tint strength varies according to manufacturer, unfortunately this is not standardised. Rather than complicate the text with a great many different names and numbers I have generalised, calling better known or commonly used colours, by name and approximate tone ie light cadmium red, dark pink, blue grey and so on.

FIRST SNOW

Support Colour, Blocking in, Blending

THE SUCCESSFUL PASTEL PAINTING RELIES on the combination of technique and a carefully chosen support colour and tone. Unless the pigment is pushed deep into the texture of the paper, (or board) the grainy quality of pastel coupled with the tooth of the support allows the colour of the support to show through as thousands of tiny pin-pricks of colour. This has a very real and dominating effect on the finished picture, so the support colour needs to be chosen with great care and consideration. Choosing correctly can cut down considerably on the amount of work needed to complete the picture and, more importantly, can make the difference between success and failure.

The choice of colour and tone can be arrived at in one of, or a combination of several ways. The colour could be chosen as closely representing the overall dominant colour of the subject, alternatively it could be chosen for being either warm or cool in colour so representing the overall colour temperature of the subject ,or it could be light, medium or dark in tone - so setting a tonal value from which to work.

Pastels are best worked broad and loosely to begin with, then gradually tightening up and working any detail in the latter final stages. Pigment can be shaved from the pastel by the rough surface of the support at a surprising rate. So use a light touch in the initial stages of the work, putting just enough pigment down to achieve the desired effect and so avoiding a premature build-up and accumulation of pastel dust in the tooth of the support.

Traditionally one of the primary pastel techniques is the blending together of colours. Whilst blending has an important role to play in most pastel works it can be overdone - resulting in a soft, flat surface without interest and impact and lacking in any sharp definition. You will find that using your pastels with clean, precise strokes and choosing your support and pastel colours with care, can keep any blending to a minimum and help your painting retain its sparkle and brilliance.

Work on a 15x22in (38x56cm) sheet of cool blue-grey paper, using white, light cobalt blue, mid cobalt blue, light cool grey, mid cool grey, dark cool grey, raw umber, raw sienna, yellow ochre and black.

MATERIALS AND EQUIPMENT

cool blue-grey paper
15x22in (38x56cm)
white, light and mid
cobalt blue, light, mid
and dark cool grey,
raw umber, raw sienna,
yellow ochre, black
fixative

The Painting

1 Working on a sheet of cool light blue-grey paper using a raw sienna pastel on its side. Begin by establishing the patch of dry bracken and grass which lies across the centre of the landscape in the middle distance. Paint in a few patches of ochre grass that can be seen showing through the snow lying in the foreground. You will find that it is often easier to use smaller pieces of pastel than large whole sticks. If you are using a new set of pastels grit your teeth and break off a piece that is ½-1in (1.25-2.5cm) long.

2 The distant bank of trees standing on the slope of the hill is lightly blocked in with a few strokes of a dark, cool grey pastel, again used on its side. With all initial blocking-in, do resist the temptation to press too hard so clogging the paper tooth with pigment too early on, which would make the application of subsequent layers of pastel very difficult.

3 With a very dark cool grey, block in and establish the skeletal shape of the leafless trees in the foreground and draw in the trunks of the few individual trees seen on the sky line.

4 Loosely block in the sky using a light cobalt blue pastel. Again use the pastel on its side to lay down the colour in wide strokes. Once the area is covered, smooth and blend the pigment over the area by rubbing with the fingers, working the pigment down into the trees.

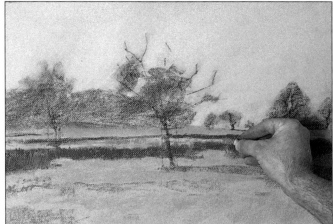

5 With a slightly darker shade of cobalt blue, loosely block in the snow lying across the far middle distance and the foreground. Once done the whole picture can be given a coat of fixative, this will have the effect of darkening the colours.

6 Work over the middle ground bracken and grass darkening the area with raw umber. Pull a little umber across from the base of the central tree to the right hand edge of the support, then rework and lighten those areas catching the light with light yellow ochre. Crisp fine lines are achieved by using the edge and the end of the pastel rather than the side.

7 A dark, cool grey reshapes, darkens and solidifies the stand of trees in the background. With a slightly lighter cool grey pull a little colour up the slope of the hill into the trees suggesting the snow that lies in the shadow beneath them. Pull a few lines of varying thickness across the foreground.

8 The dark branches and twigs are then drawn in using both a hard and soft pastel. The soft pastel easily draws in the thicker branches, whereas the harder pastel can easily be sharpened to a point and will make crisper, finer lines for the thinner branches. Alternatively use a thin piece of hard or medium charcoal for the branches.

9 Rework across the background, darkening the stand of trees on the hill and drawing in a suggestion of a few larger branches. Work the dark grey around and through the branches of the foreground trees, redefining and sharpening their shape.

10 With the light cobalt blue pastel rework the sky around and through the tree branches. If possible use a hard pastel for this as it can be sharpened, enabling you to work through and between the branches more easily.

11 With the light blue pastel on its side continue to recover the sky working down into the trees. Do not blend the pastel this time but leave the pigment lying on the tooth of the paper so allowing the previous blue layer, which reads as being slightly darker, showing through in places.

12 Using heavy, varied strokes, start overlaying the white of the snow. You can use both hard and soft pastels if you wish - the soft pastels will allow more pigment to be left on the paper giving the suggestion of deeper snow.

13 In the finished picture the combination of the paper colour and the limited palette of colours can be seen to easily and economically represent the cold winter scene.

Alternative Approaches

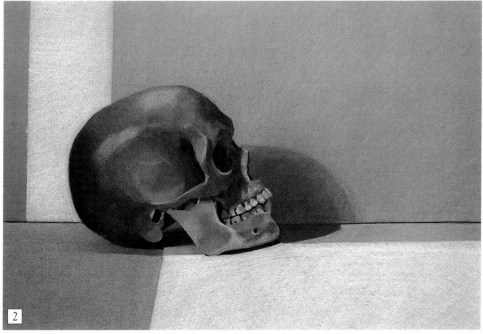

1 This relatively large painting was blocked in and the main elements established using large, thick pastels. The details were added with smaller, soft pastels and the painting fixed. Once dry the picture was reworked, again using very loose, scribbled strokes of thick pastel, especially over the foreground. The final pastel work was left unfixed so helping to retain the brightness of the colours.

2 In this tight, academic painting of a skull the initial blocking in of the forms and colours was very loose. The pigment was rubbed deep into the tooth of the paper using a torchon and any surplus pastel dust removed by tapping the back of the support, then the painting was fixed. The process was repeated many times, each time the forms and colours were tightened, modified and blended, any excess pastel removed and the work fixed.

FRUIT AND VEGETABLES

Hard Pastels and Pastel Board

HARD PASTELS ARE IN MANY WAYS EASIER to use than soft pastels, as they shed less pigment and are less prone to crumbling between the fingers. They can be sharpened to a point for detailed line work and are easily used when building up colour by cross-hatching. When broken into smaller pieces and used on their side they are perfect for the preliminary roughing out and subsequent blocking in of the composition, as they tend not to clog the texture of the support with pigment, making it possible to overlay more pastel with ease.

The materials used for this painting came from a box of short, square pastels that were extremely good value for money (they cost less than eight pounds) which shows just how little outlay you need make to begin working in pastel. The picture was constructed by underpainting using broad simple marks, this was then fixed and glazed over with more pastel, finally details and highlights were flicked in bringing the picture to life.

The choice of colour for the support may at first seem puzzling after what was said in the previous project regarding the choice of paper and board colour. However, working on a colour that is dark in tone but not strong of colour will have the effect of seemingly strengthening your pastel colours making them stand out and sparkle, jewel-like, against the dark ground. This can be especially effective with subjects that are brightly coloured, such as flowers and fruit. Brightly lit compositions also benefit from this treatment as the tones seem so much brighter when they sing out in contrast against the darker ground.

You will need a 12x16in (30.5x40.5cm) sheet of blue-grey Frisk pastel board and pastels in the following colours: white, Naples yellow, yellow ochre, dark olive green, leaf green, light leaf green, dark green, dark grey-green, lime green, burnt sienna, dark cadmium red, mid cadmium red, light cadmium red, cadmium yellow, light cadmium orange, dark orange, lemon-yellow, light grey and black.

MATERIALS AND EQUIPMENT

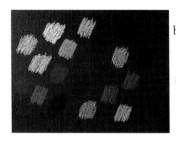

12x16in (30.5x40.5cm) blue-grey Frisk pastel board
Hard pastels in white, yellows, greens, burnt sienna, reds, oranges, light grey and black
fixative

The Painting

1 Working on a sheet of dark, blue-grey pastel board, three reds, light, medium and dark, are used to establish the colour of the peppers and tomatoes. The square pastels are used with hard precise strokes that follow the contours of the subject and the marks are left unblended.

No preparatory drawing is done but if you wish, do a faint sketch with a light pastel to act as a guide.

2 A light leaf green and a duller leaf green are used to draw in the shapes and positions of the leaves of the cauliflower and the red pepper stalks. The pastel marks are drawn using the full width of the square end.

3 The same dull leaf green pastel is used to block in the leek leaves, a darker green establishes the shadow. A few strokes of lime green are placed on the foliage of the cauliflower, then a very light ochre is used for the florets. The whites of the leeks are blocked in with broad strokes using the side of a white pastel.

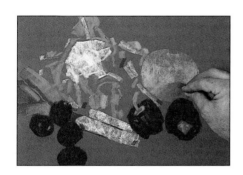

4 Turn your attentions to the squash - using the ochre, dark olive green, lime green and blue-grey fill in its shape, following the contours, but paying close attention to how the colours change on its surface as it reflects some colour from the objects that surround it. Use the same dark olive colour to paint in the shadow on and around the leeks.

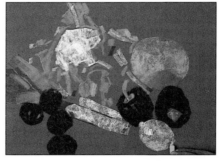

5 For the lemon, use a pale lemon yellow on the upper surface of the peel with cadmium yellow on its underside, a little white gives the highlight.

6 With a light burnt sienna glazed over with light red and Naples yellow, establish the form of the onions, then, work carefully in and around the shapes made by the other vegetables. White pastel establishes the bulb of garlic.

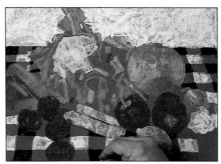

7 With white pastel used on its side, loosely block in the background, cutting around the shape of the cauliflower leaves. Then with simple, clean strokes, using the same pastel, paint in the light squares of the tablecloth.

8 With the black pastel, carefully paint in the black squares. The drawing is then given a coat of spray fixative, this will be alarming as the colours suddenly look so dull. However spraying with fixative at this stage serves two particular purposes: fixing what is there and darkening all of the colours. The picture is now reworked using the same colours which are now much brighter than the colours on the board, this simply and effectively doubles the range of colours and tones at your disposal.

9 Rework the greens on the cauliflower adding more detail to the leaves. Dark grey-green and black are worked into the shadows and white is glazed over the cauliflower florets while the colours on the squash are strengthened. Glaze white and Naples yellow over the squash following the curve of its contours.

10 Strengthen the form of the red peppers and tomatoes: pull a little Naples yellow down the leek roots, use white to press in the highlights with short, sharp strokes and repaint the yellows and oranges of the lemon.

11 The painting is now almost completed: use a cool mid-grey to paint in the grey tablecloth squares. The colour of the support is left showing through to act as the shadows that have been cast by the fruit and vegetables. The painting is left unfixed to preserve the brilliance of the colours.

Alternative Approaches

1 In this study of a cream canvas hat and denim jacket the dark warm grey colour of the support throws the hat into stark relief, whilst the bright blues used for the jacket are much more subdued. The dark support helps neutralise the brightness of the hues, making them less strident and more realistic.

2 The dark support colour used for this small sketch is made to represent the deep shadows seen on the cliffs and in the sea. A strong bright blue has been pulled across the distant sea using broad flat strokes made with the side of a square pastel, the waves in the foreground are created by using marks made with the same pastel used on edge.

THE LEOPARD SKIN COAT

Drawing and Sketching

ONE OF THE QUALITIES of pastels that makes them stand apart from other media is that they can be considered to be both suitable for painting and for drawing; the difference in definition coming simply from the application, or the way in which they are used. The majority of pastel techniques are the same as many that are used in oil, acrylic, watercolour, gouache and tempera painting. Colours are built up in solid layers, painterly strokes are used to lay opaque blocks of colour next to each other, colours are blended together and built up to form thick layers of impasto pigment, and colours can be delicately glazed over one another.

Drawing on the other hand is all about line, and pastels that are sharpened or used by their tip are well capable of making all of those marks that other traditional drawing media can make. They can produce a line that varies in quality and thickness and they will scribble, hatch and cross-hatch colours.

This wide spread of possible techniques coupled with the lack of any need for water, turpentine or drying oils and the containers to hold them, together with brushes, palettes, knives and cleaning materials, make lightweight, easy to carry pastel the perfect sketching medium. They also have an added advantage in that this duality of application coupled with the spread of possible techniques makes them very quick to use - which in many sketching situations is a very real advantage.

Working on location outdoors, capturing the fleeting variations of the weather, working at the zoo drawing animals and birds or whilst travelling on holiday, making colour notes for further reference back in the studio, planning out compositions or, as here, making quick drawings from the model, are just a few of the many situations when a small box of pastels and a few sheets of paper, or just a sketch book, are all the equipment you will need.

Work on a 28x20in (71x51cm) sheet of Not surface white watercolour paper, using white, black, pink, cadmium red, dark burnt sienna, mid burnt sienna, raw umber, cadmium orange, and burnt umber pastels.

MATERIALS AND EQUIPMENT

28x20in (71x51cm) white Not watercolour paper Various pastels in white, pink, cadmium red and orange, dark burnt and mid sienna, raw umber, burnt umber fixative

The Painting

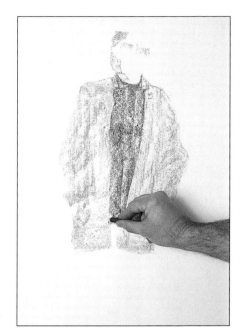

1 Working on a sheet of white Not surface watercolour paper take a few measurements so as to ensure that the proportions and position of the figure are judged correctly: you do not want to half finish the drawing only to find that the feet or head will not fit on your sheet of paper.

Using a light raw sienna pastel on its side loosely establish the shape and approximate colour of the coat with broad strokes.

2 With a medium burnt sienna indicate the dark side of the face. A dark grey pastel is then used on its side to block in the dark shape that is made by the sweater beneath the models coat.

3 A burnt umber is used on its side to establish the shape and colour of the legs. Pay particular attention to their angle, note how all of the figure's weight is on the straighter left leg. This leg is also marginally shorter, being slightly further back and behind the bent right leg.

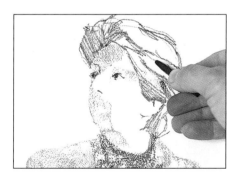

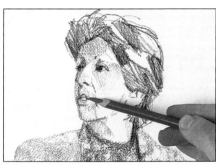

4 With a black hard Conte pastel or crayon which has been sharpened to a point, begin to draw in the hair and features. Work lightly to begin with as the harder Conte crayons are more difficult to erase should you need to correct a mistake. Once the position and shape of the features appear to be correct, the lines can be strengthened.

5 With a sharpened burnt umber and red Conte pastel, or the equivalent colour pastel pencil, continue to develop the features, working the shape of the nose and putting colour into the lips.

6 A soft black pastel is used on its side to darken the sweater. Turn the pastel onto its long edge, and by applying more pressure - redraw and darken the curve of the neckline and the creases that describe the way the sweater hangs.

7 Using a combination of pastel pencil and soft black pastel redraw and sharpen the shape of the legs together with the shoes. Shoes can be surprisingly difficult to draw, as a rule keep them simple and, if you have difficulty, merely hint at their shape by using just a few lines or blocks of colour.

8 With a combination of a dark burnt sienna, raw sienna and a bright cadmium orange block in the coloured planes that give shape to the coat, use the pastel on its side to obtain the maximum coverage on each stroke. By pulling the pastel sideways whilst holding it on one of its four edges you will get a crisp, dense line.

9 White and pink pastel give some form to the light side of the face. Then, with a burnt sienna pastel used with some pressure, establish the pattern on the fake fur coat. A few white highlights are then pressed onto the sweater.

10 Finally a white pastel is used to cut in and around sharpening and correcting the figure's outline.

11 When fixed you will notice how the colours alter very little against the white surface of the support. The entire sketch was completed in less than half an hour, and shows what a fast medium pastel can be.

Alternative Approaches

1 In contrast to the project drawing, here the figure was first sketched out in line. A minimum amount of colour, detail and pattern were then added to help describe the form.

2 The shape of a broken piece of pastel is perfect for making quick, gestural drawings that capture movement and impression. Birds and animals rarely stay still for long unless asleep, so a quick technique is essential. Here just a few strokes capture the essence of swimming penguins and provide ample information to use as reference at a later date.

GIRAFFES

Velour Paper

VELOUR PAPER OFFERS A VERY DIFFERENT surface to that offered by Ingres and the other more conventional papers. Velour papers have a soft, velvety nap that takes the pigment from soft and hard pastels very easily. These papers need to be handled and stored with a certain amount of care as they are easily marked or scuffed; the same is true when they are being used, try not to rub your hand across the surface - especially if you are wearing jewellery. Velour papers cannot be wetted and stretched like ordinary papers, neither can fixative be used on them as this dissolves the adhesive that holds the velour surface onto the backing paper. Pastel is easily rubbed off, or smeared, on velour papers so if you have difficulty keeping your hand off the surface and you are working flat or horizontally, rest the side of your drawing hand on a clean sheet of paper placed over the drawing.

However, when you are working vertically on an easel it is much easier to keep your hand from rubbing over the work, in addition the use of a mahl stick can also help. These can be purchased at most art stores, although they are very easy to make: simply cut a bamboo garden cane so that it is 3 to 4ft (around 1m) long, make the cut just above a joint. Roll up a ball of cottonwool and place it over the cut end, take a chamois leather cloth and cut a square from it, about 8x8in, (20x20cm) that is sufficiently large enough to cover the ball of wool, and be gathered neatly and tightly around the top of the cane. To secure the pad bind the chamois where it joins the cane with fine string, once firmly tied any surplus chamois sticking out below the binding can be cut off with a sharp scalpel. The slight bulge of the joint on the cane prevents the pad and binding from slipping off the end.

Work on a 16x23in (40.5x58cm) sheet of dark ochre velour paper using white, dark ochre, light ochre, Naples yellow, raw sienna, burnt umber, burnt sienna, dark burnt sienna, Prussian blue, cobalt blue, light cobalt blue, dark grey and black.

MATERIALS AND EQUIPMENT

16x23in (40.5x58cm) dark ochre velour paper Various pastels in white, dark and light ochre, Naples yellow, raw burnt and dark burnt sienna, burnt umber, blues, grey, black

The Painting

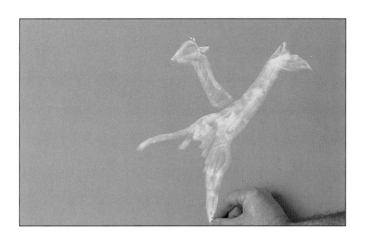

1 On a sheet of dark ochre velour paper use a small piece of soft Naples yellow pastel to block in and establish the shape and position of the two giraffes using fluid, light strokes. Very little pressure is needed as the velour paper takes the pastel easily. Corrections are very difficult on this paper so think very carefully before you commit yourself to making any marks.

2 With a small piece of light cobalt blue pastel lightly indicate the shape of the giraffe house door. Take care not to rub your hand over any pastel work already done as it will easily smudge and smear.

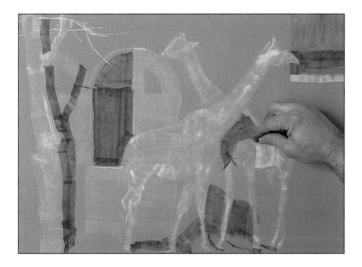

3 A yellow ochre line describes the base of the building and the darker patch of light colour on the giraffes' heads. Then Prussian blue is used to block in the sky and a light Naples yellow used to establish the shape of the tree. A dark grey is used to give the dark shadows that can be seen inside the giraffe house, on the roof of the building on the right, behind the tree and on the giraffes, use the same colour for the animals hoofs.

4 The giraffes' manes are represented by pulling down a line of burnt sienna. A dark grey line gives the gap around the doors, then a combination of burnt umber and raw sienna is used to carefully draw in the camouflage pattern on both giraffes. Note the way the pattern is distributed over the body actually helping to describe the form.

5 With a soft dark ochre pastel used on its side for maximum coverage, block in and darken the giraffe house wall.

6 With black pastel darken the pattern on the far giraffe's neck together with the pattern in the deep shadow on its front. Intensify and darken the colour inside the giraffe house and draw in the shape of the window glazing bars. Also darken the giraffes shadows and the roof on the right hand side.

7 Add a little detail to the tree; then with small pieces of square umber and sienna pastels draw in a suggestion of the brickwork.

8 Return to the giraffes and rework the light areas between and around the dark pattern with a Naples yellow pastel. Pull some colour down to strengthen the colour on the spindly legs.

9 Lighten the door surround with white and use it again on the belly of each giraffe. Drag a little light blue across the foreground to give a suggestion of the compound floor.

10 The painting is completed by adding Naples yellow details to the brickwork. Burnt umber adds a little bark to the tree and the sky is made lighter with the addition of cobalt blue.

Alternative Approaches

1 Short pieces of square or round pastel used on Mi-Teintes paper make establishing the elephant's shape and colour fast and easy. The same pastel used on edge delivers a feint, fine or thick heavy line depending on the pressure. None of the colours are blended - this keeps them crisp and bright.

2 This study of macaws was made with large and fast gestural strokes utilising the side of the pastel.

This can best be seen on the wing and tail feathers where the pastel is used on its side and turned as the stroke is delivered to make a fluid, feather-shaped mark. Animals can be awkward to draw unless the action is frozen by taking a photograph, working from birds and animals in captivity is always good practice as many of their actions tend to be repetitive.

ROUSSILLON

Sandpaper and Impasto

I FIND FINE SANDPAPER to be one of the most ideal surfaces for making pastel paintings on - it is extremely pleasant to work with and its fine, regular tooth easily takes marks made by soft pastels, hard pastels and pastel pencils. It will allow most techniques to be used, including reasonably delicate fine line work, subtle glazing and the build-up of heavy impasto, and gives a look to the finished work that is perhaps most like that achieved when oil paint is used on canvas. Its only major drawbacks are that it cannot be worked on using water or water based paints as these dissolve and break down the adhesive that keeps the sand in place on the backing paper and the fingers can become sore after heavy blending and rubbing on the gritty surface.

Fine sandpaper is available in various grades, the finest is 00 grade and is known as flour paper, it comes in a neutral buff colour and can be found in art shops. Hardware stores also stock sheets of sandpaper in various grades and colours along with emery paper which is almost black in colour and is used for polishing the surface of metals and alloys although it can also be used as a surface to work on. The two slight disadvantages that paper bought from hardware stores have, are the size of the sheets available, which are invariably small, 11x9in (28x23cm) and they are not made from acid-free materials. This means that given time, the colour of the pastels may be affected; that said, they are perfect for sketching, experimenting and the working out of ideas - in other words when the longevity of the work is not of primary importance.

The secret of successfully working on this type of support is to build the work gradually, avoiding too heavy a build-up of pastel too early on. Do preliminary work with the harder pastels and pastel pencils, if possible leaving any heavy impasto work with the softer pastels until the final stages. Erasing marks, however, can be a problem - limited success can be achieved by using putty rubbers, blue tack or even masking tape which if rubbed down over the pastel will remove some of the pigment dust when peeled away. Excess pastel can also be removed by using a stiff bristle brush. By far the easiest solution is simply to work over any mistakes with thick layers of pastel.

Work on a 30x22in (76x56cm) sheet of 00 grade flour paper using a selection of white, Naples yellow, yellow ochre, dark yellow ochre, terracotta, burnt sienna, burnt umber, raw umber, dark grey, light blue-grey, cerulean blue, cobalt blue, Prussian blue, light green, dark green, light pink and black.

MATERIALS AND EQUIPMENT

30x22in (76x56cm) 00 grade flour paper Use soft, hard and pencil pastels in white, yellows, browns, greys, blues, greens, pink and black.

The Painting

2 Continue to work across the street until all the buildings are established. Use the black pastel to lightly scribble on tone over those areas that are dark and in deep shadow.

1 Begin by sketching in the tower and buildings with terracotta, Naples yellow and black pastels. Work lightly so as to avoid an early build-up of pigment dust clogging the tooth of the sandpaper.

3 With a light cerulean blue pastel used on its side, block in the sky and the blue shutter in the side of the building on the left. Darken the building on the right a little and the dark doorway at the base of the building on the left. Then use burnt sienna, burnt umber and ochre pastels to establish the overall terracotta colour of the same building.

4 The bell tower is blocked in next using a mixture of Naples yellow raw umber and dark grey scribbled on and blended together using the fingers, draw in the wooden shutter on the window using dark grey. Establish the position of the bushes seen through the archway with light green. Scribble dark grey over the road and darken the shadow beneath the arch with Prussian blue and more dark grey.

5 Block in the pink door with terracotta and darken the wall of the low building on the right with burnt umber and burnt sienna; the shadow from the roof is darkened with burnt umber. With dark grey colour in the doorway on the right and the arched doorway on the left. The colour of the wall that can be seen through the archway is established with burnt umber and dark grey, then a small piece of black pastel is used to block in the dark shadows seen beneath the eaves of the building on the right.

6 Finish blocking in the dark building on the right with burnt sienna and black, then fix the whole drawing. Using white, cerulean and cobalt blue rework the sky with short hatched strokes of thick impasto colour. Begin by painting in the white clouds then work around them with the two light blues.

8 Light blue-grey, Naples yellow and ochre are glazed in layers onto the tower. Naples yellow also adds a few light accents at the top of the tower and around the bell - pull some of the same light colour down the top of the wall that runs to the side of the steps that ascend up to the bell tower. Then with a sharpened hard black pastel draw in the details on the tower, bell and clock.

7 With the black pastel darken the roof line and windows on the building to the left. Draw in the line of tiles with burnt sienna and the details on the blue shutter; then with a darkish yellow ochre and burnt sienna pastel dab on some heavy marks across the wall. With the Naples yellow pastel lighten and define the stonework around the dark doorway on the left.

9 With Naples yellow, highlight the sill beneath the shuttered window on the tower. Cerulean blue is used for the light path seen through the arch and a white line describes the sunlit top of the wall. The walls of the buildings are then blocked in again using Naples yellow.

10 With square burnt sienna, Naples yellow and light pink pastels, use short strokes with the square end of the pastels to describe the shape of the tiles seen on the roof.

11 With thick heavy strokes using a raw umber pastel paint in the stonework on the right hand building using choppy, short strokes. Work over this with the lighter yellow ochre pastel to indicate where the light hits the stonework.

12 The picture is completed by adding some blue-grey stonework to the same wall. Add a few Naples yellow accents to the wall seen through the archway, and finally, indicate the shadows on the shrubs with a little dark green.

Alternative Approaches

1 This painting of Stonehenge utilises the grey of the paper to represent the local colour of the stonework. Thick impasto pastel was built-up in layers for the landscape and sky and torn paper used as a mask to give the edge between the light and dark green grass in the foreground.

2 A watercolour underpainting laid the foundation for this pastel of a beach umbrella and sun loungers - once dry the watercolour was worked over with heavy pastel which takes easily to the rough texture of the watercolour paper.

FLOWERS

Building an Image

FLOWERS HAVE BEEN A popular subject for the artist since the sixteenth century, whilst having been included in many works before that date they had never been thought of as a worthwhile central subject in their own right. Since then most artists, for one reason or another at some point in their working life, turn their attentions to flowers - doubtless attracted by the huge variety of forms and colours. Pastels are particularly suited to painting flowers as the purity and brilliance of the vast colour range seems to match that of the subject - open a box of pastels and they seem to shout 'flowers'. Look at a florists stall and it is as if you are looking at a display of pastels in an art supply store.

As with the fruit and vegetables in Project Two, this painting of a bunch of mixed flowers that have been apparently carelessly plonked into a modest glass jam jar, has been done on a dark paper so as to allow the colours to sing out. The painting was made using a mixture of strokes and techniques and a variety of hard and soft pastels, no blending took place - rather the colours were placed with precise, clean strokes over or next to one another.

In this particular painting the hardness of the pastel was not of any significant importance, each pastel was chosen primarily for its colour. The picture was made by slowly building a framework of carefully considered marks relating each to the other until the form of the flowers began to read correctly. The final flower and leaf shapes are drawn and redefined by cutting in and around with the background colours, carefully working the negative shapes.

Work on a dark green 29x21in (74x53cm) sheet of Canson Mi-Teintes paper using white, dark grey, light grey, dull green, bright green, lime green, bright pink, purple, cobalt blue, cerulean blue, dull orange, bright orange, alizarin crimson, cadmium red, burnt sienna, cadmium yellow, lemon yellow and Naples yellow.

MATERIALS AND EQUIPMENT

29x21in (74x53cm) dark green Mi-Teintes paper Charcoal. Pastels in white, greys, greens, blues, yellows reds, oranges, browns, bright pink and purple Fixative

The Painting

2 Continue to create a frame-work of shapes and colours using mainly the mid tones, ignoring the highlights and darks for the moment. Gradually the image evolves and comes into focus as the simple blocks of flat colour start to relate to one another. Light grey indicates a few reflections in the glass jar and a burnt sienna pastel is used to draw in a flower stem.

1 Working on a dark green paper begin to establish the shape and position of the flowers using small pieces of pastel that are as close in colour to those colours seen on the subject. The positions of the first few marks are very important as everything else is related to them. Do not press too hard at this stage as the intention is to lay in just the ghost of an image that will provide a foundation and guide for further work. A light grey pastel indicates the shape of the glass jar.

3 The process continues, now turning attention to the very dark greens and blacks; these are worked carefully in and around the mid-toned brighter flower colours showing the position of those leaves and flowers that are in deep shadow.

4 Tight intricate areas are picked out using a sharpened charcoal stick to draw around and through the forms - cutting in and redefining their shapes.

5 As the dark blocking in continues, the flower shapes are seen to emerge from the dark green paper and the image is almost complete. Still using a black pastel, or stick of charcoal, begin to indicate the negative spaces between the flower stems seen through the jar; then using a black pastel on its side, block in the dark wall behind the jar, together with a few of the shadows that can be seen to fall across the cloth.

6 The painting can now be given a coat of fixative. Once the paper is dry a light blue-grey pastel is used on its side for maximum coverage to establish the light wall to the side of the window.

8 Strengthen the light grey behind the flowers and scribble more Naples yellow into the vertical strip running down the centre of the painting. White picks out the shape of the daisies and the other flower colours are strengthened and shapes redefined using clean precise strokes using a range of red, yellow, and purple pastels. Once this process is completed give another coat of fixative.

7 Single strokes of Naples yellow and burnt sienna establish the frame of the window, whilst cerulean blue loosely blocks in the blue outside. With white, block in the tablecloth leaving the colour of the paper to represent any shadows. Once done the painting can be refixed.

9 The background is reworked and the colours in the picture intensified, some cobalt reflections are put on the glass jar. Strengthen the stalks with green and the vertical strip with burnt sienna. The colours become slightly duller each time they are fixed, enabling the same colour to be used in layers, each one appears to be a different shade or tone. This is most obvious on the daisies and other flowers.

10 A few bright green accents on the foliage and the stems seen through the jar are made with a lime green pastel. The vertical dark line on the wall behind is drawn in with the end of a square black pastel; work also by darkening between the flowers, the stems and through the vase with black pastel and charcoal.

11 Finally paint in the highlights and the tablecloth with heavy but firm strokes.

12 The finished painting has a brilliant jewel-like quality with the bright colours working hard against the dark colour of the support. Had the painting been done on a paler paper the intensity and brightness of the finished image would have been reduced.

Alternative Approaches

1 Heavy impasto applications of pastel built the foundation for this painting of a swimmer. The painting was well fixed before more pastel was glazed over the surface creating the subtle differences of tone and colour seen in the disturbed water. White was finally used to give the pattern of ripples and the mosaic of tiles that can be seen through the water on the base of the pool.

2 This landscape in Tuscany was painted using large thick pastels to scribble on the pigment; fixative was used between layers, not just to fix the work but to 'knock back' or deaden the colour. This technique enables the same colour to be used several times on top of itself, each layer looking like a brighter version.

PENGUIN POOL

Pastel on Marble Dust Board

FOR REAL DEPTH OF COLOUR AND A surface that allows far more layers of pastel to be applied than is possible on paper, there is no substitute for a board prepared with acrylic gesso and marble dust. Preparing the boards is simplicity itself and their very nature makes the act of working in pastels more closely related to painting than it already is. The rigidity of the board also seems to be reassuring and gives the work a feeling of permanence and stability that can sometimes seem lacking in works that are done on paper.

The boards can be prepared using thick card, hardboard or medium density fibre-board. MDF is available in various thicknesses, is very stable and not prone to warping or bending, the surface is also able to stand up to quite rough treatment making it possible to scrape out work and make corrections. Any marble dust surface that is also removed in the process can be renewed by sprinkling on more dust and spraying with fixative to bond it onto the surface. Marble dust can also be added as you work in order to increase and vary the tooth in different areas of the painting.

One more advantage of working on board is that it enables the artist to employ the technique, used in this project, of mixing and working into the preliminary layers with a liquid medium, this can be either spirit or water based. With spirit based mediums such as turpentine or white spirit the pigment is spread easily but darkens appreciably, this can be no bad thing and once dry gives a stable surface ready for further work.

Water mixes and spreads the pastel just as easily, the colours also become dark when wet but lighten again once dry. I mix a little acrylic matte medium with the water which mixes well with the pastel and dries to give a stable surface that will not smear as it is worked on. Several layers can be built up like this but care must be taken not to add too much acrylic medium or it may clog the tooth of the support.

Work on a piece of MDF that has been prepared using acrylic gesso and marble dust. Use white, light, mid and dark cerulean blue, cobalt blue, Prussian blue, dark turquoise, black, dark green, pink, light green-grey, and cadmium yellow.

MATERIALS AND EQUIPMENT

MDF board prepared with acrylic gesso and marble dust
Fixative Torchon
Pastels in white, blues, greens, turquoise, yellow, black and pink

The Painting

1 Work over the marble board with three blues: cerulean, light cobalt and Prussian. Use the side of the pastel for maximum coverage and speed, there's no need to cover the board. completely. The three blues, light, medium and dark are positioned on the board to roughly correspond with the light, medium and dark areas of water.

2 Mix up a little acrylic matt medium with water and, using a large flat brush, scrub over the surface loosely blending the pastel onto the board. If you're working vertically don't be concerned if the mixture runs, this will be covered by subsequent work. Allow the work to dry before continuing, the process can be speeded up by using a hair dryer.

3 With a sharp, hard black pastel draw in the shape and position of the penguin. Work the pastel heavily over those areas that are very dark and lightly scribble a little pastel onto the lighter area of the penguin's back and the reflection of the head that can be seen in the water.

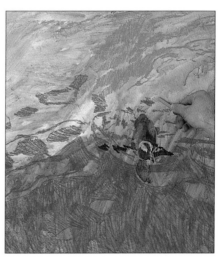

4 A little white is added for the light plumage on the top of the head and around the eyes, some more white is scribbled onto the back and, using a torchon, blended with the black to make a grey. Add a little pink above the eyes and smooth out the white on the head with the torchon and fix.

5 With a dark turquoise pastel work over the dark reflections seen in the foreground and around the penguin. Use a loose open scribbling technique. Do not try to completely cover the board with opaque pastel or the surface will become clogged with pigment, and try not to work too literally as there is no need to paint in every last reflection and ripple.

6 Work the mid blues in the same way using the same open scribbling technique, add a little grey into the ripples that spread out behind the bird.

7 With the very pale blue block in those areas of water where the reflections are at their lightest. Already the illusion is beginning to work: the water has depth and the penguin appears to float comfortably on the surface.

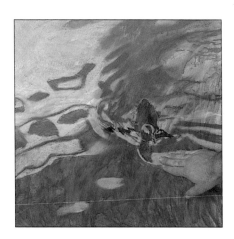

8 Once the blocking in of the water is complete the scribbled colours are roughly blended and smoothed. The fingers are used for the larger areas and a torchon for small, intricate areas around the penguin. When this is done the painting is given another spray of fixative.

9 Darken, sharpen and redraw the shape of the penguins' wings beneath the water using black and dark blue pastel. Carefully observe how the ripples fragment and distort the part of the bird beneath the water.

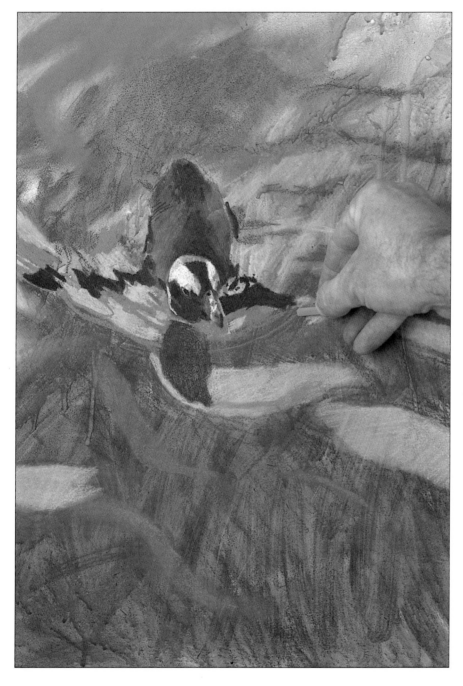

11 The darker cerulean blue is pulled across the painting in fluid wavy lines describing the effects of the light coupled with the movement of the water. Blend with the fingers or the torchon to remove any crisp hard edges and then fix again.

10 Add a patch of white to both sides of the head just above the eyes and a few white accents on the beak. Then, with a dark green, deepen the colour seen in the reflection of the head and using a dark cerulean blue carefully paint in more of the ripples around the bird.

12 Rework and darken the deep blue, work in layers smoothing out the pastel as you go until the right depth and density of colour is achieved.

13 Light blue and white pastels are then used for the sparkle and highlights on the water. The light blue is used first to establish the delicate tracery of small ripples, followed by the white which is applied thickly using heavy pressure to leave a lot of pigment.

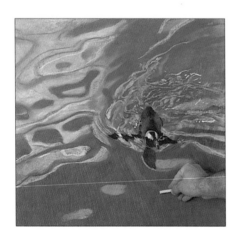

14 The picture is completed by using a hard cadmium yellow pastel for the mosaic of tiny tiles on base of pool: notice how the water distorts, magnifies and curves the straight lines of tiles.

15 In the finished painting it can be seen what a difference the tiles have made - all of the work until the final stage had been about representing what was happening to the surface of the water - with the introduction of the distorted tiles on the pool bottom suddenly there is an illusion of real depth.

Alternative Approaches

1 Done on a sheet of hardboard (masonite) prepared with marble dust and gesso, this small landscape of a Tuscan hillside was done over another painting which I was unsatisfied with. By adding more marble dust then fixing, and by working in layers of opaque pastel it was possible to work on board without leaving a trace of the previous painting, something which would have been extremely difficult to do on a paper support.

2 This painting of a little girl was done on a sheet of watercolour board prepared with marble dust, the image was established using watercolour before being finished with hard pastels to heighten colour and develop the details.

PORTRAIT

Drawing with Pastel Pencil

IN ALL OF THE PASTEL WORKS THAT HAVE been reproduced in this book so far, apart from Project Three, line work has been kept to a minimum or is virtually none-existent. The pictures have been completed using solid applications of colour, invariably without any preliminary drawing, using glazing and impasto as well as various traditional painting techniques that are more readily associated with oil or other painting media that use either oil or water based mediums as vehicles to carry and spread the pigment.

As we have mentioned previously, pastels are unique in that they fall between two stools, being both a painting and a drawing material - using techniques taken from both disciplines. Soft pastels are capable of line work but far better results will come from using hard pastels, or pastel pencils, which will allow solid areas of colour to be made, but are put to better and more economical use when used for line work.

The ability of pastel pencils to switch from making solid blocks of colour to fine intricate line work make them an extremely versatile medium. They can be used on all of the traditional textured surfaces that are used when working with soft pastels, with the added advantage that they are clean to work with. Pastel pencils deposit less pigment onto the support, so whilst it is possible to blend colours with the finger or torchon, better results will come from using those methods that rely on the density or spacing of the line work as seen in scribbling, hatching and cross-hatching techniques. The openness or linear quality of these techniques also allows for considerable amounts or layers of overworking, as the pigment dust takes far longer to build-up and clog the tooth of the support than it would if solid blocks of heavy colour were used.

Work on a 25x20in (63.5x51cm) sheet of beige or buff-coloured paper using white, Naples yellow, pink, cadmium red, burnt sienna, burnt umber, cadmium orange, dull green, cobalt blue, dull cerulean blue, light cerulean blue, bright pink and black.

MATERIALS AND EQUIPMENT

25x20in (63,5x51cm) buff paper
Fixative Torchon
Hard and pencil pastels in white, red, yellow, browns, blues, orange, green, pink and black

The Painting

1 Working on cream paper begin by taking a few measurements, making sure the proportions are correct and that the figure sits comfortably in the picture. Lightly map out the position of the figure using black, burnt sienna and orange pastel pencils, so any lines that are positioned badly can be redrawn without needing to erase.

2 The position of the features are redefined and corrected. Tone is scribbled onto the face showing the position of the shadows and a suggestion of form - the lips are drawn using cadmium red and the shape of the hair is redrawn and the eyes darkened with black.

3 With a black pastel, scribble a little colour onto the model's top then work over the skirt blocking in the direction and position of the patchwork pattern using an alizarin crimson pencil.

4 Draw the fall of the hair with firm strokes of black and then scribble some of the same colour over the background shadow and the hair. Darken the eyes further and draw in the dark area seen inside the slightly open mouth. Lightly scribble a little dark blue into the background shadow, then again using the black, block in the models top.

5 With light green, cobalt blue and cadmium red establish more of the skirt's patchwork pattern, then using Naples yellow, light pink and white begin to work up the mid to light tones with a series of hatched and scribbled lines. The whole image is now well established and can be fixed.

6 Once the fixative is dry return to work - consolidate the dark colours and tones on the face, sharpen the features and darken those areas in deep shadow with hatched and cross-hatched lines using cadmium red and burnt sienna. Establish the shadow that curls over and down the left arm using red, burnt sienna and cobalt blue. Still using cobalt, hatch onto the side of the forehead and nose and over the shadow on the leg.

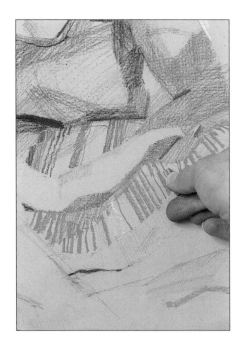

7 Introduce more colour into the light and mid flesh tones by cross-hatching more Naples yellow, pink, and white. Then intensify and deepen the colour in the deep shadows surrounding the features.

8 With black and cobalt blue darken the shadows on the wall behind the subject, then rework the model's top using varying pressure to indicate the contours of the fabric and the underlying form. Note how the dark line that is drawn across the midriff helps the figure to lean forward.

9 Using a combination of blue, bright pink, sienna and red hard square pastels and pastel pencils draw in the lines of the pattern that cover the skirt.

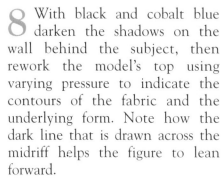

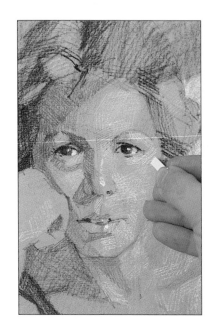

10 With a hard white pastel block in the sunlit wall behind the figure; as with any large area of scribbled colour or tone, change direction frequently so that the scribbling does not lead the eye in any one direction.

11 Finally a hard square Naples yellow pastel is used to hatch and cross-hatch highlights onto the face, arms and legs.

12 In the finished picture the use of scribbling and hatching from the pointed pastel pencils have lent a much more open linear quality that makes the work readily identifiable as a pastel drawing rather than a pastel painting.

Alternative Approaches

1 Methodical light grey cross-hatching reverses the figure out of its background. In particular note how the leopardskin coat is represented by the colour of the support with only the shape of the pattern giving it form.

2 Seen contre-jour, or against the light, this simple study of a woman's profile was done using just five pastel pencils. Again the careful and considered choice of support colour has cut down on work.

INDEX